The Gentleman's Guide to Romancing

Your Woman or Significant Other: 11 Inspired
Dates Sure to Impress...
That Won't Break the Bank

DL Smith

Disclaimer

The author does not guarantee that any of the suggested dates will provide you with the experience you want. These are only suggestions and recommendations for dates. Additionally, products recommended in the book may be suggested with affiliate compensation to the author. It is not necessary to purchase these products, other similar products may be substituted for the suggested ones if you so choose.

The Gentleman's Guide to Romancing Your Woman

or Significant Other: 11 Inspired Dates Sure to Impress...

that Won't Break the Bank/ DL Smith, First Edition

ISBN: 0-9772-8885-4

Contents

Introduction

First off, let me thank you for your purchase and spending your hard earned money with me. I feel far too often we take you, the customer, for granted and do not effectively communicate our sentiments of gratitude. Secondly, you might ask yourself why there are only eleven dates in this book, is there a reason for this? Yes, this is only installment one, with the success you will realize off just this one book I am confident you will be back. Moreover, if you can spent a couple bucks to get tips to wow and impress the woman of your dreams, I think it would be more than worth it; call it money well spent. Moving on.

Scenario: its 7:33 on a Friday night, you're sitting on the sofa with a bowl of lasagna in your lap, your diet Coke is nearby while Steve Harvey cracks jokes on the Family Feud. This is nothing unusual, in fact it is your typical Friday evening. Why, because you're a slouch, a couch potato, a loser or a slob? No, it is something much deeper than people understand.

You must realize you are not alone in your struggle. Nearly one in two men is single according to the 2015 US Consensus Report. That's half the population of available men. Of those, how many of us do you really think have the tools, confidence, chutzpah or swag to play the dating game in 2016? Very few, trust me.

There must be a thousand or more articles written about the affect social media has on dating life, or "lifestyle" but the lifestyle isn't so great if there are no dates to be had. True, the landscape has changed from what those of us over 35 would most recently call a "date"; however, the foundation of the relationship has not. I find we allow media to dictate how we date, how we communicate and our expectations. We set a low bar for standards in how we pursue dating, lessen our options because the odds seem stacked against us and we tend to skip over what was once the most important thing about dating – impressing the date.

I will share personal accounts and anecdotes to illustrate how you can better your own personal situation or learn from someone else's. There is no one right way to do anything when it comes to dating but there is a way to discover what can and will work for you. Understand, your clumsiness in fumbling the date isn't all your fault, many of us simply haven't been taught – blame it on your mom! How's that for a Mother's Day sentiment? Seriously, it's like anything else if you don't have a point of reference, haven't seen it in real time, had any exposure or training the only way you can learn is from trial and error, otherwise known as "practice".

Here's a thought, have you ever seen that person out in a Starbucks, LA Fitness or the grocer and felt an immediate attraction to him or her? Perhaps 7 times out of 10 that person was made up or dressed nicely, right? Or, maybe he or she had a nicely toned or shapely body, no? So, that person you're gushing over has your attention but you are too shy, afraid or apprehensive to approach them. Let's address this.

That person you are day dreaming about is just another human being, like you. He or she has feelings, ideas, pain, hurt and everything else you have. In fact, they may have the same butterflies you have in the pit of your stomach at the possibility of meeting you. Who knows, maybe you're a pretty decent catch yourself! But, consider this – how much time would you think went into the preparation for that person to look the way they did? An hour? Maybe two? Weeks? Months? If the person is a fitness buff, they probably work at sculpting their body regularly, watch their weight and their diet, none of which is an easy task to maintain long term. If he or she is a fashionista, then you know they spent time in front of the mirror fixing their hair, face and outfit to look good for you.

What am I getting at? Preparation. Everything requires some amount of preparation and I am convinced the more preparation you are equipped with in this market, the better you can play the game; if you play the game with a well designed playbook, your odds at winning increase dramatically. Best of all, I will walk you through creating a memorable date leaving her with a huge smile looking forward to the next. We will also address a few things like timing, pressure, etiquette and the like just to fine tune your skills for even better results.

My goal will be to take a man, or woman, who lacks dating prowess or the confidence to navigate a positive date. Part of dating is getting past the first date, otherwise it isn't dating it's just a string of first dates, which can get pretty expensive and grows old quickly. Now, if your aim is to pick up some tips on how to score this book is probably not for you, not that I'm against "scoring" but this one is for people who want to learn how to romance their significant other. I'll work on putting together that book as well, maybe another volume (smile).

Finally, I will share one of my most prized talents – the art of mastering a memorable date on a budget; after all, it is no secret a series of first dates can easily bust your budget or break the bank. And no, I'm not talking about meeting up at your local Starbucks or indie coffee shop. Unfortunately, they are hip to that game, it's tired and it's played out, so let's get you some new options and get things back on the right track. What do you say? If that's a yes, I'll see you on the next page.

Chapter One

Picnic in the park

Anyone who knows me from my online persona would tell you I am a pretty creative person, which threads into my personal life often. In thinking back on my life experiences I do think I've had my share of some pretty amazing and unique things to happen, such as getting married on a sandy white beach in Ocho Rios, Jamaica under the bluest skies you could possibly imagine. Or snorkeling with sting rays, yes I actually did that. Or climbing the steps of one of the ancient pyramids of the Mayan Ruins, it was a little scary but fun. And yet having done all these things, for the most part, I can relate to the average guy pretty well, especially coming from a small rural community in the South.

While I live in a metropolitan city now, I certainly realize this is not going to be the case for many of my readers. In today's global marketplace I expect there will be readers from other countries who find themselves in the same plight as any other man in any other part of the world struggling to please his significant other. If you knew me personally, you would also know I prefer to keep it simple. So let's do just that and start with the basics.

Recently, I spoke with two of my best guy friends who found themselves in the proverbial dog house after Mother's Day. Both are married and both screwed up royally. For the sake of ease, I'll label them as Buddy #1 and Buddy #2.

Four days before Mother's Day Buddy #1 found himself behind the eight ball financially. He told me about how he was sitting at the stop light when steam came from his engine suddenly. Moments later he was in that place where we have likely all been but no one wants to experience, his car overheated. After a 45 minute wait on the roadside, his car was towed to the mechanic only to learn he had a blown head gasket. His bill was astronomical!

Trying to juggle two young children, one teen and one college age child, Buddy #1's budget is strapped with little room for error. Now, you and I would probably agree he should be given a pass on those merits alone…not so with your Mrs. Instead of putting forth any effort in doing something special for his wife, he chose to buy a cheap, cheesy card from the local 7/11 on his way home from work. No flowers. No jewelry. No new car, well maybe the new car would be extreme but definitely needed under the circumstances.

When we spoke he was insistent he had done nothing wrong and wanted my perspective as a pseudo relationship pro – I don't know if I'd go as far as to agree with that but I have a pretty keen understanding of women. My first question to him was why did he only purchase a card for her and nothing more? His answer was simple; he didn't have the money – a seemingly innocent enough response.

Do this; ask any women who has birthed four children for her husband if she is okay being forgotten, or that is how she will likely frame it, on the designated special day for moms. With the sheer amount of commercials spent on the holiday alone, we men are stuck if your budget doesn't permit you to do something on a semi-grand scale. So as you might expect, a measly card isn't going to do it on her day; hence, the visit to the dog house!

While I believe every woman should be wined and dined, catered to, so on and so forth, I also believe a lot depends on a man's budget, financial circumstances and his willingness to spend his hard earned money. An inherent flaw in dating, first dates in particular, is the man is expected to spend his money to cover the expense of the date, which would be okay if the first date lead to something more long term. In that case it could be considered an investment as the two of you are getting to know each other and most men don't mind making the investment, within reason, to establish that kind of relationship.

But, the unfortunate place we find ourselves in today just doesn't support that notion any longer. Today, first dates are not as common as they once were. As mentioned, there has been a seismic shift in how dates are made and had which leads to more first dates and less second dates. In other words ladies the response you're getting from men who want to "Netflix and Chill" is partly due to these guys consistently shelling out money and not seeing the relationship go anywhere.

That all said, I do not think it is necessary to break the bank, as is mentioned in the title. This is where some creativity comes in to keep from coming off as cheap. One such date, the first we'll explore, is a picnic in the park. Now, I chose this date to begin with because everyplace has a park, that's not specific to any region, country, etcetera. It also eases you into the mindset I want to help you establish and gently nudge you in the right direction.

Before we dive in to the good stuff, let's take a moment to discuss the elephant in the room – open your ears and listening. Yes, I said it; and yes, I am on your side but you must understand in order to be an effective lover you must learn to be a better listener. The strategies, techniques and tips I will offer are not intuitive – or at least not to you or else you wouldn't have purchased this book. But being a better listen isn't as simple as just sitting back with your mouth shut, nope, you aren't getting off that easy. Is this starting to sound like a pain in the rump? Probably. But keep reading, you can thank me later.

Being a good listener means you are actively listening. Understand, for the most part, she isn't likely talking just to hear herself talking; we may think that but rarely is that the case. Indeed, maybe she is venting and if that's the case, let her vent; better that than the alternative. But maybe, just maybe, she's giving you the ammunition to target her heart. She's sharing small bullets of information you can use to impress and wow her, why? Just because you cared enough to listen and actually pay attention. In my experience, often times your woman just wants the respect of being heard.

What is "active listening"? It's just as it sounds…active, being engaged in the conversation. Ask questions to let her know you are engaged. Some examples of questions you can ask that will benefit your dating experience are:

What kind of wine do you like?

What kind of cheese do you like? Do you like brie?

Is she the outdoors type?

Does she have allergies to pollen, the sun, freshly cut grass, etc.?

Next, we begin the planning. It's always nice if you can coordinate your picnic with a special event like an outdoor jazz concert or something. But let's assume you cannot, we begin with the basics. I suggest a large cloth bag (for durability) to sack the items you will carry. The simplest thing to do is to fix cold cut sandwiches, bag up some chips in a couple zip locks, pack up a few bottled waters and add her favorite wine. In your preparation you will need to include plastic cutlery, plates, condiments, cups and a means to carry/ keep ice. This may all sound like a lot but trust me it is fully worth the effort once you get to your destination and set up.

On that note, you tend to get what you put into it. What I've described so far is nothing more than the basics in establishing a romantic date. If you want to take it to the next level, you should invest in a wicker picnic basket, which start around $35.00 (order: http://amzn.com/B00L4EJQ88). These baskets are amazing and super impressive to even the most sophisticated woman as they have nice plastic glasses, dishes and typically metal cutlery. They are spacious and really give a polished look to your picnic outing. Trust me when I tell you that you will be the envy of all the couples around you.

As you plan for your outing, be sure to pack up something to spread across the ground. There is nothing worse than planning for a nice date but she won't participate because she doesn't want to get her nice outfit dirty, can you blame her? Personally, I recommend beach towels as they are multipurpose, soft, and comfortable; also, they wash easily (order: http://amzn.com/B017XL4K5O).   I like to pack up some fruits like strawberries, blue berries, and blackberries, cut pineapple or whatever her preference is.

Remember, this date isn't about you, it's about her. As long as you keep her wants at the forefront of your thoughts you will put yourself in the best position. Maybe she doesn't drink wine, that's fine. Bring whatever she likes to drink, and it doesn't hurt to bring something for you as well. A side note: do not bring hard liquor on a first date. There is nothing sexy about your drunken mannerisms because you can't handle your liquor. Let's get past the first few dates before she sees that side of you.

In preparation, you can create a playlist or pull up your favorite streaming site on your phone if you require music to set the tone. I would suggest stopping by your local grocer and pick up one single rose to accompany your meal. For added shock value, you can pull it out and present it to her when you open your new picnic basket. By the way, one thing I often do is order food from a restaurant for the picnic. You don't need to pretend you made it; rather, just leave out early enough to stop and pick the food up, then pack it into your basket before you get back in route to your destination. This way she won't be waiting on you and you'll get high marks for your preparedness. Oh, and don't forget the bottle opener, which is always a losing proposition (order: http://amzn.com/B019DNPU8G). For the record, we will come back to Buddy #2 later in the book.

Chapter Two

Be a Foodie at the Food Truck Park

What were once branded as "roach coaches", these fast food joints on wheels are now all the buzz. That's right, it's a truck and it sells food. What kinds of food? All types of food; tacos, burritos, pizza, burgers, seafood, fried stuff, baked stuff, candied stuff and even slightly weird stuff. In fact food trucks have become so popular that in many cities there are entire areas where a number of trucks collectively park and sell their food. These areas are affectionately known as food truck parks. Indeed, food trucks have come a long, long way from 10 to 15 years ago when it was less than desirable to order from them.

When I think of food truck parks, I tend to think of urbanites, hipsters, millennials and couples with pizzazz. Of course we know that isn't necessarily the case but what is certain is a good food truck can give a popular restaurant a run for its' money. I have had some great experiences at food truck parks. But there are pros and cons though; again, a little planning goes a long way.

Once you're armed with the information on what she might enjoy food-wise, when she's available and you have a target date in mind, I would perform a simple Google search for "food truck parks" in your area. Typically you will something come up, most have their own website complete with a list of dates for specific events – that's right, these places have their own events to attract more customers.

A side note, I would recommend checking your planned date against the weather forecast. If there is even a chance at rain I would recommend taking a large umbrella, better safe than sorry. And there is nothing worse than ruining the perfect date with poor planning. In fact, if a women has recently spent $100 bucks or more on getting her hair done you might find yourself in hot water by not planning better in case of rain.

Here's a perk you might like: as mentioned, most food truck parks have events, especially during the summer months. One thing I like to do is bring along a nice bottle of wine (yes I am a wine drinker), a couple lawn chairs and sit back in the grassy area listening to the live bands play. You can find out when live bands will be playing in your area. In essence you get two high quality activities for basically free. You might wonder how they do it but as I am told the vendors chip in a small fee for the live entertainment – it's a draw.

Another tip, one way to spruce up the experience even more is to order in the amount of tapas. Tapas are Spanish appetizers, when they are ordered in a restaurant they're usually served in a way that the table or couple can share. Actually sharing is encouraged. Imagine a few plates of samplers, these are tapas. I say take a page out of the playbook of the Spanish. Visit several food trucks, order small sharable quantities and have some fun along the way.

Again, I have to address the elephant in the room. This time it is the "stiffness" lots of you guys have. Look, no woman likes a stiff, stuffy guy. When you're out on a date let your hair down a bit. Loosen up your collar, drop the corporate lingo and relax. Let your personality peek through, show her a little of who you are. Are you a movie buff or a comic nerd? Are you a bird watcher or secret, undercover foodie? Share a little about yourself, or better yet...

Remember, you asked those questions to learn more about her? How about using that information to find an area where you two relate to each other. For instance, she told you she has a thing for men in uniform. You use that information to let her know you were once in the military or you may crack a joke telling her you're wearing your uniform under your clothes – you're quietly a superhero! Sounds corny, sure, but it breaks the ice.

Your goal is to get her to open up, talk and share. But how you accomplish this goal is you must be open yourself. Work hard to avoid awkward pauses, they are the death nail to second dates. How I do this is to point out interesting things in the crowd like people, specific vendors, vendor's names, discuss something about the area of the city, be current on local affairs and news. This will show you have the ability to keep her interest that goes a long way in getting a second date.

Also, be complimentary, women love to receive praise, especially for their look. Recall in Chapter One we discussed how many women will spend lots of time planning their look to impress you. Show her you are impressed, it's okay to be vulnerable. Compliment her shoes, her skirt, her blouse, her jacket, or even better yet, her smile. One thing to note in dishing compliments is to be authentic. No one likes a kiss ass for the sake of trying to "get some". She can tell, and you know when you're not real.

A quick story, I remember the first time I went to a food truck park many years ago. It wasn't as planned as I am instructing you to be; hence you can learn from my mistake. I was going out with a model for whom I would describe as "metropolitan". She was this leggy, very chic person with a cute British accent. She wore heavy red lip gloss and flats (shoes) because she was six feet tall. In her flats we stood nearly eye to eye, me only a half inch or so taller than her. We met during a brief encounter at the local airport. Her travels were to someplace exotic, mine was to visit family in the Bible belt. Needless to say I felt I needed to step up my game to impress her.

One of my friends told me about this new thing called the food truck park. I figured why not? It was something different; it would make me stand out from all the other douche bags trying to win her over with their money. And, it gave me an opportunity to pick her up so we could be in the car together. Call me old fashioned but there is something to be said for riding in the car together – small talk, building rapport, establishing a connection, etc. For many first dates these days you might find yourself meeting up; anything you can do to position yourself in her company more, all the better.

The date went pretty well. She had never gone to a food truck park either, so the experience was new and exciting to the both of us. There wasn't anything going on entertainment-wise other than people watching, and that's just what we did. Things were going smoothly until a soft wind began to blow. That should have been our queue it was time to go but we were each caught up in the moment. Time seemed to stand still as we star gazed…then the first drop of rain fell. Within mere minutes we were drenched trying to make our way back to my car. I remember the feeling I had in my gut looking on at the better prepared guys with their extra large umbrellas covering their women from the cold rain.

Back at the car we climbed in and sat momentarily. It was scene from a Rom-Com (romance comedy), we sat in silence then began laughing – hard! There was a sea of brake lights illuminating the only street exiting the park; we weren't going anywhere anytime soon. Lucky me! She was so impressed with my choice of the food park, the conversation and my lightheartedness about the rain dampening the evening that we made out right then and there! It was one of the most memorable experiences of my life. I'm not going to pretend you will make out in a food truck park with a model too. Nor, will I advocate the lack of preparation that just happened to work out for me; rather, what I will tell you is if you implement any of this suggestion into your dating blueprint, you will realize favorable results.

Chapter Three

The Rooftop Lunch

Let's face it, we live in an instant gratification, no frills society where little emphasis is put on making anything special anymore, especially dates. Don't believe me? Then ask yourself why apps like Tinder, OkayCupid, PlentyOfFish and others so hot right now. There was a time when it was the guys who were only looking for a hookup or one night stand; that time is no longer. Today's woman is prolonging starting her family well into her 30's, if even at all. I've come across many women who are forgoing having children for the self indulgence of being able to live life on their own terms and not be beholden to the confines of having a family. That would be an interesting case study.

On that note, sometimes a colloquialism applies such as "get in where you fit in", meaning that you take advantage of the opportunity when it presents itself. True, not all first dates are under ideal circumstances. And depending on the woman, the demands of her job or her travel itinerary, you may find yourself competing with some unseen forces. And worse, if you haven't had the opportunity to make your mark or impression, she won't give a second thought at waiving off your advances leaving you on the outside looking in. So how do we correct this issue?

Ever met that person who strikes your fancy, and maybe they share a little interest in you too – or at least as far as you can tell through a quick call or text? You've tried the coffee thing (again, that's played out fellas), you've tried to hint at a happy hour, you've even tried to offer to pay for lunch, all to no avail. What I am about to propose is not for everyone. Let me reiterate this point to drive it home, this date requires you to be a little ballsy. Why? You're about to find out.

Let say the only time you can catch your heart's desire is at her job; she's a work-a–holic, eats, sleeps and poops work. And you insistent she's the one who changes your life. Okay. Well, everyone has to take lunch, nothing new there. But what if you take lunch to her where she works? If you approach it correctly, who can say no to a free lunch brought to their doorstep by a man trying to woo them? Before you get all negative on me, keep reading.

The approach I would take in this scenario is to politely probe the receptionist for the company's, or departments, lunch hour. If you really want to play dirty, go in and win the receptionist over. Use your million dollar charm on her to gain a valuable alley. If she seems receptive to your charm, share with her what you are trying to do and see if she can help you. She can run interference and help set the stage but conveying a message or something along those lines. I have purchased blank greeting cards that allow you to write your own message. Write a simple message asking her to meet you in the parking lot or at the top of the parking deck for a special surprise. Curiosity is in people's nature, this will be a hard one to resist.

Note, do not be cheap. This is not the time to allow your frugality to ruin your chances at getting your foot through the door. Additionally, if you aren't a poet by nature or you don't have a creative bone in your body, may I suggest a friendly visit to your local Hall Mark store (or even the card aisle at Target for that matter), pick up a few cards, "borrow" some lines and make yourself sound a little better than the average Joe. But you didn't hear that from me, I do not condone plagiarism but…sometimes "you've gotta do what you've gotta do" – another applicable colloquialism.

Order a lunch for two from a nice local restaurant if she's that type, or when in doubt. If she's more of the blue collar type, pick up something that would impress her still; at least spring for Applebee's two for $25.00, she's worth $12.50 I hope. And as much as I hate to say this as it would seem to be commonsense, I've learned there is nothing common about commonsense, leave the alcohol at home. No wine. Or at least, not this time. Remember, she's on lunch so water is preferred.

Now, your instruction in the card needs to be crystal clear; any ambiguity can and will trip up your entire plan. Before you tell her where to meet you make sure you've already secured a park. Can you imagine if she takes you up on the offer and you can't find a park in the space where you've designated? The next thing you know you've just hooked up Johnnie with your woman. Crap happens.

Also, your message in the card should be fairly succinct (short). Going back to the point about instant gratification, people are not readers anymore. If it has more than the allotted Twitter characters, your message may not get read. And that would be a bummer!

Let's just say all goes according to plan, she comes out to meet you, what then? You need to understand a few things:

She will have a limited amount of time.

You had better have a heck of a game plan to get her to stay.

If she gets the wrong vibe you will be forever labeled a stalker.

If you play your cards right, you will be the envy of the office.

Notice, there is a common theme in each date thus far…planning. In your planning would you park your car in the hottest, sunniest spot on the lot? Of course not, that would be poor planning at its worst. You should park somewhere away from traffic, in the shade if possible and maybe slightly private. If she uses a parking deck, or you're required to use one, park on the rooftop they are rarely busy; no one wants to take the time to walk down several flights of stairs or wait on the elevator.

When she arrives the very first thing you should do is thank her for taking time away from her lunch break to have a quick bite with you. Show appreciation for her willingness to give you a shot. Next, ask her about her day, about the card, about what she thought of your offer/ action, all while you prepare the meal. Work quickly, multi-task so as to not waste any of her time and your precious time in getting to know her better.

Another nice gesture that will earn you browning points and light up her eyes for days is, if she has children ask about them. Only women with bad kids will not want to talk about them, otherwise, you'll likely touch on a soft spot that will earn you additional browning points. Ask her to show you a picture of them on her phone. She will likely pull them up from her social media account and when she does ask if you can connect with her. Take that moment to connect with her on the spot, don't wait and let it potentially pass.

Not that you're a stalker or anything like that but you can learn a lot about someone from their social media profile. Again, the more you know the better equipped you are in knowing how to please her. I often hear women say they want men to be more intuitive. And since men typically have problems expressing our feelings anyhow, intuition is not going to be our strong suite. But this is how you make that connection.

Now that you've impressed her with showing interest in what she does, shown you're a good listener and even inquired about the kids, easily back away. What? Did you just say back away? Don't I go in for the kill? No. Women want what they can't have. Case in point, have you ever seen a parent play with a toddler, they hold out their hand and when the toddler goes to smack it they quickly pull their hand away. It infuriates the toddler and they want to do it again and again until they catch their prey. The same applies here, not that your date is a toddler but the principal is the same.

24

As you wrap up, you can lean in for the kiss, if the opportunity is right, but kiss her on the cheek. If you kiss her in the lips, don't linger, make it short and sweet. And most importantly, you must initiate the close of the date. Women like an Alpha male. Act as though you're one, even if you're not. In this case, learn to take control when it's needed for the sake of portraying strength. You can blow it here if you come off soft and weak. Whereas it took some guts to pull off the stunt you just did, it takes even more confidence to close it down when the other person is feeling you. But, if you want to remain in control and increase your chances of a second date, it is necessary.

Thank her for her time, ask her if she'd like to meet you again and if so let her know you will be in touch soon. This will kill her with anticipation as she awaits your call. In a primal sense, everyone wants to feel needed. And everyone loves the thrill of something new and exciting, and you my friend just provided that for her, you lucky dog you! By the way, if she's the "selfie" type, this is a perfect opportunity for some great selfies! Encourage it – why not, she's going to look back at them and reflect on a moment with you. How's that for winning?

Chapter Four

Star Gazing

Growing up in the rural south as teens we were forced to be more creative when dating because there simply wasn't much to do. I remember there was a hill in the local park where everyone always went to "talk". What I remember most about that hill is how we would lay in the back of an old pick up and star gaze.

Star gazing, you city folks may be asking yourself "What is that?" It's just as it sounds, when you stare into the night sky looking for constellations, shapes, stars, clouds or anything that may pique your interest. Perhaps this is the cheapest date you could imagine, right? But, let's pretend you can get past the cost, or lack thereof, for a moment and let me explain how this can work for you.

First off, there is one thing that is absolutely bankable with this date – no rich guy will ever think to do this as it would be considered silly and offensive for him not to show off his wealth. Now, even most regular would probably take a pass on this one for fear of being too cheesy. But on that off chance you have a lady who appreciates something different, think how she may be more receptive to you after you've shown her something new that she has always taken for granted like the rest of the so-called civilized world.

Again, to make this work it all goes back to what? Preparation. I would recommend pulling up an astronomy or constellation app. Sure you can do it while you're on your date, and that's okay but having the app already on your phone or tablet gives you that extra edge.

In your preparation, locate a quiet place preferably on a hill, a field, an empty parking lot or a rooftop where there is clear visibility of the night sky. You should also check the local forecast as your plan will be ruined if there is overcast or rain on the night you go out.

It should go without saying this is not recommended for a first date however. This date requires some established trust and rapport as it could be a turn off to do something so intimate on a first time out. You want her to have a comfort with you that she would not mind spending the quiet time with you.

Understand, the idea here is to get her alone from the hustle and bustle of the usual "date" stuff like restaurants, movies, etc. This is an opportunity to expose your lighter side, allow her in and give her a chance to get to know your quirky sense of humor, your charm, your geekiness or your intellect. Are you an avid reader? Yes? Well do you think you'd have a chance to talk about the latest book she's read during a movie or a concert? Probably not.

You see so often we acquiesce to what everyone else does not trying to stand out or do anything to separate us from the herd. There is certainly safety in the herd but if you want to impress her you will hardly leave an impression doing the same things everyone else does. You may argue that you want to play it more conservatively on a first date. Or you've never ventured beyond the "norm" so this would be out of character for you with your significant other. And that's probably true but I can also tell you that shaking things up a bit is more often than not just what the relationship needs. Between kids, work, bills, bosses, in-laws, etc. it's a full time job to keep your lady happy, why not make it interesting?

Again, being armed with the answers from the questions you asked in your information gathering session (please be tactful) you will know if she is amenable to alcohol. Wine or wine coolers would be appropriate here if she enjoys partaking of spirits. Personally I enjoy chilled wine such as something fruity like a Pink Moscato, Riesling,

Sweet Red Merlot, White Zinfandel or a Port wine. Avoid the cheap stuff, no Boone's Farm. A decent bottle will cost under $20.00 at your local grocer but a terrific buy and great option is the variety pack listed here at under $60.00: http://amzn.com/B012SF0UQI.

I recommend packing up a blanket or beach towel so that if the moment is right and she feels a bit more adventurous you can roll with it. For the guys who have no clue what I'm talking about, here's a simple hint, go here and just buy it: http://amzn.com/B018727EQK. You might find yourself under a hickory tree with the moonlight peeping through as she lays confident in your arms. This is a prime example when it's not all about sex. Yes, this seems like the perfect place for a sexual encounter and if it goes there then great. But what separates you from those other guys is you know your patience, control and will power gives her a strange appeal toward you she can't quite explain.

If you can maintain control she will be the instigator and you will find yourself "messing around" when you didn't have to be the aggressor. That is a win-win for everyone, you get what you ultimately want and so does she – respect, compassion and being heard. So call off the dogs, put your testosterone on hold, let the evening take shape naturally. It will unfold slowly, easy. Relax, be carefree. Talk about everything, talk about nothing, talk about what's important to her but I should caution you…stay away from politics, religion or anything else that can kill a great date!

The last thing I will say about star gazing, I remember once in college I rented a high powered telescope for a date. Upon picking up my date I asked if she trusted me, of course she said yes. It was sort of late when we were getting together, like 10 pm. By then I knew she would have likely already eaten but I was equipped with a secret weapon. I learned from her roommate she had a thing for barbeque pork rinds and Diet Dr. Pepper, go figure!

We drove to the top of the parking deck for the library, and yes she thought I was completely crazy for a moment, until I got out of the car. I placed two lawn chairs in an empty parking space, took out the telescope and asked her to join me. As she did I offered her the bag of pork rinds and a bottled Diet Dr. Pepper. I think she lost it for a second. She literally leaped into my arms, kissed me and backed away before I had a chance to process what had just happened.

The date was so smooth, so easy and just flat out fun. It was the start of a great relationship. She always told me I won her over from the first date by doing something so simple as to show up with her favorite guilty pleasure. Trust me when I say your woman has a guilty pleasure too. Who cares what it is if it puts you in a positive light with her. We are not here to judge, the objective is to learn how to please her. If you haven't noticed, it is not always the grand, over the top gestures that get you the most credit with them. Mostly they just want to be acknowledged and shown some attention. And they want to be heard, which is why I continually put you in a position where you can LISTEN, respond but also share too.

Chapter Five

Discover Your Local Museum

It is probably safe to say most men do not think to visit the local museum without some prodding, poking or flat out being told to do so. Heck, I'm not judging, I'm guilty of it too. Now, being a student of the arts I probably have a greater appreciation of local museums than the average guy. But even I can say they can definitely be boring and a little on the snooty side, and that may not be your thing. But, hear me out before you tune out.

In any given city or state there are any number of museums to be discovered and explored. The key is to find one that piques your interest and hers. For example, say your date is into American history and you are a fan of the Confederacy, you do realize there are a plethora of Civil War museums just waiting for you to show your patronage, right?

Or let's say your first date was to see The Fast & The Furious franchise. You learned she loves muscle cars like you. You happen to live in Bowling Green, Kentucky where there is a Corvette museum (see: http://www.visitbgky.com/visit/coupons-discounts/) awaiting your arrival for a pretty cool follow up date. Or maybe she's a movie buff and you are too. You live in an area like Atlanta where there is a movie tour (see: http://atlantamovietours.com/) for some of the major movie and television productions that have been shot there in recent years.

Finding that right fit for your local museum tour is just a matter of finding the right fit for you. Have you ever wanted to go to Madame Tussauds Wax Museum (see: https://www2.madametussauds.com)? If you haven't you should, the attention to detail in their work is amazing!

When you figure out what is an appropriate fit for you, you should plan your date around it. This is a scenario when you would want to Google restaurants in the area where you can dine with your date before or after the tour. You should also check the website of the museum so that you know their opening and closing hours, especially their closing hours as you do not want to accidentally miss the showing. Again, a lack of preparedness can speak as loudly as being prepared and the date going off without a hitch.

Or how about a themed event where you both dress according to the venue to spruce up the date a bit? An example of this might be a train museum tour where a Western theme might be appropriate (see: http://www.srmduluth.org/museum.html). You tour may be complete with a local train ride in an antique train car. And in many cases retired cars are turned into restaurants for patrons of the museum to enjoy. How often can she say she's experienced that? Probably not ever.

I'd like to reiterate your objective; your goal is to do something different than the norm, work to stand out and separate yourself from the pack. This applies even if you're married. Can you imagine what she will say about you to friends, coworkers and family if you blow her mind with your thoughtfulness and fortitude? Better yet, do you think any of this might have a positive effect on your intimacy in the bedroom?

Another elephant in the room moment; gentlemen, please understand every relationship – married or otherwise – requires that you continue to date your woman. I would highly recommend establishing "date nights" if you haven't already. It's a way of saving you a world of headache when you've ignored your spouse for too long and her feelings change.

I speak from personal experience as a man who goofed up and didn't show his wife the attention she required. Separation, divorce, counseling – it's all troublesome, heart wrenching but most of all…avoidable! But we have a role to play in keeping our women pleased as much as possible, hence the reason you're reading this book.

Gentlemen, in some rare instances you may run across a woman who is not necessarily a romantic and that's okay. She may be a sports fanatic, knows players stats better than you and can put a ball through a hoop like Steph Curry, great! Can you imagine if you took her to the Basketball Hall of Fame? Or what if you arranged a tour of the CNN building in Atlanta during a taping of "Inside the NBA" with Shaq and Barkley just a few feet away? Do you think she would be even slightly impressed?

While I cannot say I have visited all of these places, I can say each of them has merit in their own right. Women, like us, have many different interests. Do not assume that just because she's a woman she wants to do something soft and flowery when that may not be the case at all. She may enjoy a trip to the Hard Rock Café where she can get a taste of Rock'n'Roll in a stroll down memory lane. Or she may be into paleontology and enjoy an exhibit of ancient artifacts, fossils and dinosaur skeletons. One thing is for sure, do your homework if you want optimal results.

A real life case study: a good friend from college, remember Buddy #2? So, Buddy #2 told me how he met his wife and what he did to win her over. Like many people, as a working professional with two children by a previous ex he found life to be hectic and overrun with debt and burdens. He didn't have time to date or even try to date because he was working 50 + hours per week and finishing up a second degree at the same time. So, at the advice of a fellow friend he began online dating.

What started as a means of simply having some innocent companionship in talking online lead to calls, which led to a date. Buddy #2 had gathered information that his date was a fan of Beyonce and as it so happened he knew she was shooting "Fighting Temptations" at an old warehouse in Atlanta. Coincidentally, his date loved architecture and warehouse districts like the one where the film was shooting which provided the perfect cover for an incredible surprise.

His female friend lived near the Georgia – Tennessee border and was desperate for some action in her life. After a little coaxing he convinced her to drive a couple hours down the interstate to hang out with him. He made her a promise it would be a date she would never forget. The only thing was he required she come early, bring a change of clothes in case they went dancing and be prepared for a long day. That's a curious request, right? But she obliged him.

A few days earlier, through some sleuth-like detective work Buddy #2 had learned of a casting call for extras (see: http://www.tourgeorgiafilm.com/article/how-to-become-an-extra) in the Fighting Temptations movie. His plan was to meet his date for an early breakfast then take her to the movie set where she just might catch a glance of her idol. Now if you don't know anything about movie sets, it really isn't as glamorous as it's made out to be. Shoots are made up of long, tiresome days filled with retakes and lots of sitting around. Luckily for Buddy #2, when they arrived at the set and his date discovered what they were doing and why she was there, she had no complaints.

The building was a historic warehouse district with wood beams and rot iron railings sure to impress his date. Needless to say she was enamored with the building's architecture, it had the impression of a museum, which is was Buddy #2 was going for. But in this case he got the element of surprise with the building, the movie shoot and they would make a few bucks, a nice three for one!

As luck would have it, Buddy #2 and his date just so happened to fit the look the director wanted for a particular scene. And with the change of clothes they each brought they fit right in for this once in a life time role! They were chosen to be in the dance scene with Beyonce and Cuba Gooding Jr. In fact, they danced so well they were placed near Beyonce and Cuba whereas they could be clearly seen on screen during the scene.

Call it fate, or call it luck, but what happened with Buddy #2 is a terrific example of how a little (or a lot of) planning and probing can go an awfully long way.

Chapter Six

Top Down, Easy Day Drive

Fact - most of us live an entirely too stressful lifestyle. We're pumped up on all sorts of medications to keep us moving but rarely stop to smell the roses. Well here's the thing, roses die too. In other words, the opportunity doesn't last forever. So you ask yourself, what am I getting at?

When understanding romance, a very large portion of romance is slowing down, unwinding and going with the flow. That, for many of us, may sound like an impossible task. Life is happening all the time. Ball games, recitals, work, vacation, weddings, funerals, etc. all come into play. And yes, we all have them but we cannot give in to those demands or our lives aren't ours anymore. It happens.

As you learn to tap into your romantic side, you will need to learn to simply slow down. Romance isn't hurried or rushed. It isn't on a time clock. And you cannot turn it on and off like a light switch. It is time you invest into your partner, learning what pleases her. Imagine knowing her so well you can surprise her with something she will love that she's never considered doing before. Indeed, many, if not most of these tips, I would say most women have experienced only a few times in their lives. Why? Because they are so simple they're taken for granted. If you plan your romance according to TV advertisements you will see it's all about spending money, and lots of it – how else would those ads be paid for otherwise?

While in college, I once dated a young lady from Dakota – North or South, you pick, I really don't remember that specific detail. As mentioned, I am from a rural part of the country and we did some really silly "country" stuff. Like what you ask? Well, like "crusin"; yep, I said crusin! It was like a scene straight out of Footloose. All the local high schoolers would hop in their cars and cruise up and down Main Street for hours on end on a Friday or Saturday. Of course it was a car show for kids whose parents had money; they drove the "hot" cars. But a little nobody like myself, I was proud of the pennies I pulled together over a couple summers. You wouldn't believe my first car was a black 1968 Cadillac hearse, but that's a story for another day.

So crusin' was our thing but she taught me an important lesson in deconstructing stress. I remember it was just after finals and I was stressed to the max. We hadn't received our grades yet so the pressure was on. In fact, my scholarship depended on it. I had goofed off for a few weeks during the semester so this particular final's was of the upmost importance to me. She saw my frustrations and felt the stress on my shoulders. She suggested we do something I had never thought to do…take a ride.

As simple as it sounds, it was the most relaxing thing I had ever done. Okay, you're ready to tune out, right? Hang in there, give me a few minutes to explain and clarify. Surely by now I've earned that amount of trust?

So yes, it is as simple as it sounds with one big exception – it is intentional. She said, "Let's get away! Let's go for a ride down the interstate and see where it takes us." I loved the thought of something as carefree, unbridled and freeing as doing nothing but driving. Gas prices were low and the interstate was calling, there was only one thing to make it even better. I rented a convertible.

With the top down, a bag packed with a quick change of clothes and a tank full of gas, we were on our way within a couple hours. We ended up in the Smokey Mountains, about 4 hours away, rented a log cabin for the night and had the best one day trip I can recall. Unlike the other dates to this point, this one requires less planning. But, if you're like most people, some amount of planning is still necessary to keep the ship moving back home.

One of the things I liked best about this date is what you learn about a person on the road. Sure, if you're married or in a long term relationship you've been in the car together on many a day; you've likely taken road trips, short or long, together at some point. What's different is you don't have a set destination. Imagine with resources like www.Airbnb.com where you can book a room on the fly, you can now get the sense of living in a small town, city or beach community.

I'd recommend a playlist to impress her. Sure the radio is okay, or a CD is slightly better but how about a playlist to set the tone and mood? How about fun songs, upbeat, whatever that makes your hips wiggle? Do you know what she likes to listen to? Then all the better, go for it. I can't tell you just how many occasions in my life have been set to a soundtrack. Often I will be riding down the road only to hear a song from the 90's come on and take me down memory lane for an experience I had with someone I was dating at the time.

Understand where you are, you are creating your "memory lane" with her. It's important to walk in the moment, savor it, let it wash over you and cherish it for the precious time it is. We only get so many of these experiences in our lives. Sure, go ahead, laugh but ask any divorced man who is now without his home, his kids, his life and his wife – ask him how corny the idea of being carefree and living in momentary bliss sounds when life is much harder. Most divorced men, me included, would tell you there were things we could have done to help save the relationship. I am no marriage counselor but I can say from experience it's the simple things we ignore or blow off that mean much more to them than you can ever imagine.

Chapter Seven

Sandy Toes

Okay, remember in the title I said these were dates that wouldn't break the bank? Well yeah, this one can definitely be a bit pricey but certainly worth it if you have any time invested with your significant other already. This isn't a first or second date type of thing but it is a date that can go a long way in getting you out of the dog house.

Do you recall the first time you had the experience of sand underneath your feet, squishing between your toes? Maybe it was wet and stuck to your feet. Or maybe it was dry and dusted your feet and legs like fine powder. Just beyond the sand in front of you was a rolling beach or shoreline leading to large body of water, most likely the ocean if you were lucky. The tides drifted in causing you to sink deeper in the sand but you don't mind because it feels so good. Do you recall that? Yes? Well that's the experience I want you to give to her, and let's discuss how you do it.

Like every date we've discuss thus far, planning is a must. Of course you have the scheduling situation with work and time off, that's a given. But if you plan smart you can save yourself tons by booking ahead. If you know the only time you have off is during the next holiday, you should give yourself as much lead time as possible. I'd recommend 3-6 months. This is ample time to book a nice room, condo or beach house. Booking agents and property managers tend to offer better deals and rates to people who book in advance. The closer you get to the date of choice, the more you will pay; it's simple supply and demand. So procrastinating will be costly, I don't advise it if you can avoid it.

Another thing I recommend is subscribing to travel sites for discounted updates. There are a number of large sites but there are a few smaller sites I recommend such as Jet Radar, see: http://www.jetradar.com/?marker=54671. By being in the know on what deals are available, you can better plan a get away to a nearby beach or trip to the islands of choice. Either way you save money which you can use to spend on wining and dining her, I'm sure she will not oppose that.

The elephant in the room: when you get away…actually get away. What I mean by that is leave your work at home. If you're in sales, self employed or you're a contractor, I get it; if you don't answer the phone money doesn't come in. But, remember this is a vacation of sorts and she will expect you to break away from the hum drum you're both accustomed to. If you must, set aside a couple hours in the morning to return calls and emails but do it quickly so as to not interrupt your time together. Again, the objective is spending time together. Make the effort, it will pay dividends.

This next suggestion is totally up to you but take heed if you really want to maximize the opportunity and time you have to get away. Look into a VRBO's (vacation rentals by owner) for nice little cottage or house on the beach where you can walk out the door and have sand in your toes within minutes. Look for something exclusive, remote or non-touristy. Why? I think you'll find more things to do with your time than eating out or doing the same things you would do at home if you're challenged to do so.

As the dusk sets in, the tides quietly wash up to the shore, take her hand. Lead her into the sunset walking side by side in your favorite linens or whatever is comfy. Take your time, stroll, it's not a race; you're not in a rush. Remind yourself you have no place to be. Stop, allow the water to swirl around your legs. Pull her in closely and kiss her tenderly reminding her of what you have together.

This is the moment that sets up the rest of the evening. It is the foreplay turning on her mind without ever removing a stitch of clothing. You may want to take her right then and there, if you're on a private beach I say go for it! Or you may want to take it a bit slower and tactfully build the tension. Take her back to the beach house where you have pineapple, strawberries and blueberries waiting with her favorite wine or beverage.

Lay her back then use the fruit to accentuate the moment. Feed her the fruit. It can be playful. It can be serious. It can be mouth to mouth so your lips touch and your tongues meet. You can place the fruit along her body while nibbling at her skin as you eat each bite. Be curious. Be adventurous. Be bold.

Probably the most important thing to know is women want us to take charge. Do not wait on her to initiate the moment that would be a grave mistake and turn your trip into a Shakespearean tragedy. Now, it is fully possible she will initiate the engagement since you have shown her a tender side that she probably hasn't seen much of. If that is the case, roll with it; if not, be smart and don't ruin the moment by being awkward and clumsy in handling her. Touch her with confidence, know that she is yours and you are hers.

If it's been a while, and I've been there too, take it slow, women typically do not want to be rushed. It tends to ruin a good moment. I know you may be ready but have you done everything you need to bring her to that point? Does she require more verbal exchange? Does she prefer heightening her senses with your touch? Is she a kisser? Does she want you to talk dirty or play dress up?

I do realize some of my suggestions may seem like common sense, but we know what we've established about common sense by now. If this doesn't apply to you, kudos to you; for the rest of us, if you apply these tips I promise you will have an interesting evening at the very least.

Chapter Eight

Bubbles, Bubbles, Bubbles…and Candlelight

What is romance exactly? It is a subject open to debate. And certainly what is romance to one isn't necessarily romantic to another. Romance in my mind is showing your softer side. It doesn't mean getting in touch with your "feminine" side as a male; rather, it does mean opening your mind to allow yourself to tune into what a woman wants, what she appreciates and what she needs.

To understand this difference in men and women is to better understand this chapter and how it can benefit your relationship. Often we men assume our women should simply understand us, or just get out of the way. In the way of emotions we tend to be very practical, or what you might call "black and white". But this is a common fallacy that plays out in every race, creed and culture as I've come to learn in my 43 years.

With women, the more of their senses you can appeal to the better the overall experience will be when you are trying to win them over. Romance begins in their heads; you have to turn them on mentally. Yes, it does seem like a trick because how can you know what she's thinking? Simple. Ask. I too was guilty of making this mistake for some time. But when I finally learned, it clicked. I would argue and complain about not knowing what she was thinking when all the while she just wanted me to inquire about her thoughts and what was near and dear to her heart.

To set the stage for this next date, we will use the element of surprise. No doubt, many of you have never even considered doing this for your women. If you have, you probably didn't do it right. If you did do it right, you probably haven't done it in a very long time. And if you past that test, then why are you reading this book? Get the drift?

So let's start with, what have I been preaching? Preparation. Every one of you has a bathtub. Some of you may have a garden tub with the jet streams, if so, nice! Others may have the basic ol' white tub. And even others of you may have the more stylish and modern "throw back" or "retro" tubs that are stand alone in the middle of the floor; again, a slick look. But this date does not require anything fancy. What it does require is appealing to her next sense…smell.

If you haven't noticed women love candles. They'll spend hundreds of dollars a year on candles. Do this, first buy a small bag of tea candles from your local grocer. Next, purchase a nice scented candle. Women love 3 wick candles, and I prefer them because they last a long time and they're great value for the money. There are a number of places you can go but if you are unsure what to get, go here for a great product by Bath & Body Works: http://amzn.com/B005O91CUE.

Other products you will want to have on hand are bath salt (see: http://amzn.com/B01AKW4378), and some type of bubble bath like Calgon. If you want an all in one solution, a set that has everything you will need – and will make you look like a stud – you should pick up this one and be done with it: http://amzn.com/B00658O82M.

Another thing I recommend are rose petals. Are they absolutely necessary? No. Are they a nice touch? Yes. Hell yes! Remember the goal here is to wow her. And I know I said these dates will not break the bank but don't be a cheap skate over a few extra bucks on a bag of rose petals. The extra bang for the buck you'll get out of a few well placed rose petals will be immeasurable in return.

Now, for the element of surprise, you will need to know her schedule. Plan it out so that she is not home or she's home and preoccupied while you set your plan in motion. You might even get help from the kids, a friend or relative to run interference for you so that you can pull it off successfully.

Draw a hot bath in the tub while pouring in the recommended amount of bath salt. I'm sure a lot of you are wondering what's the big deal about bath salt, right? Let me explain, have you ever had a strained back or leg and you took an Epsom salt bath? Well it's similar, except that it smells really good and the bath salts are designed to remove even more toxins than the Epsom salt. It will make her skin silky and soft to the touch.

Add a dash of bubble bath to the water. Don't add too much because, as I've discovered, most bubble baths for adults are pretty concentrated and will bubble up nicely with just a few drops. Anything more than that will probably cause her to itch, that does not bode well for your desired result.

While the water is running, set the mood with the tea candles. Place five or six strategically around the bathtub but away from where yours or her head might rest. Place your big candle on the sink or in your bedroom if it's nearby. If it's in the bedroom it will be a subtle hint at there's more to come. Speaking of which, subtly is key here. Don't be overbearing, relax and just go with the flow.

What about the rose petals? Sprinkle a few in the water, sprinkle a few on the ledge of the bathtub and sprinkle a few atop your bed. No need to overdo it. Another nice touch is her favorite wine and favorite fruit. You might recall this from a walk on the beach. Did I cheat here, I don't think so. While it's the same on the surface, it's not the same. Why? Because it's not the same to her; the setting is different, the place is different, the effort is different.

Another nice touch to help set the ambiance, play some soft music in the background. Go down and invite her into your snare. Be sure

47

the lights are off and the candles on when she walks in. Her eyes will light up and she will be so beside herself she won't know what to do.

Time for another story: I recall my last year or so in college I dated a young lady who was one of the most sensual people I would ever meet. She turned me on to so many things in knowing how to please women. She was probably the first woman to explain to how to make love to her, what a woman finds pleasurable and what she doesn't. Its mind blowing, trust me! Oh, and we'll get there in the next book.

Now, I considered myself a romantic before I met her; I mean after all I had coasted through college just fine with the women I dated. None expressed any complaints. But if you think it's about not getting complaints then you miss the point entirely.

I will never forget the day she asked me to draw bath water for her. I did, then she stepped in. She asked me if I would wash her hair. Gentlemen, believe me when I tell you that if you want to leave an impression on your significant other…wash her hair. I know it sounds like the simplest thing in the entire world, and it is, but that is what they want from us.

I washed her long, beautiful hair for the first time and it was a sensual experience for the both of us. It turned me on in ways I didn't expect and couldn't explain. As for you, use a sponge and wash her body. With her eyes closed, softly squeeze the sponge dripping water across her back, neck, breasts and lips. That is what builds the sensuality in what might otherwise be considered mundane.

When she exits the bath, she will be completely relaxed and putty in your hands…be careful to keep the mood in tune with what you have created. Don't bring anything into the conversation other than meeting your end goal. If you have "swag" now is the time to use it. Say whatever comes to mind that you think she will want to hear. Remember, at this moment you can do no wrong. Use it to your advantage and help ease her mind so that she can enjoy the experience fully.

Chapter Nine

Take Me Out to the Ball Game

On to America's favorite past time, yep you guessed it…baseball! Or, let's just say a sporting event she enjoys. If she doesn't have a preference after you've done your research, then you choose one. Don't over think it, you aren't signing a million dollar contract with the Dodgers. You goal is to pick a game, any game, where you can get her away from the bustle of life, let her hair down, maybe drink a beer or two and have a good time. That sounds good, right? So let's discuss how you get there.

If you live in a rural area there may not be an opportunity to take your significant other to a professional sports game, or even college for that matter. But guess what, that's okay. When was the last time you went out to a local high school football, baseball or basketball game? You'd be surprised at how much action there is on a Friday night. Without question it is the highlight of many

people's week. Now, if you're a sports family already this is probably not the right option for you, keep reading. As for all others, keep this in mind and make the necessary adjustments as I further explain how to apply this technique with professional sports.

Let's pause here for a moment. I know some of you are asking yourselves what's so special about a ball game? Well if you haven't been, you wouldn't know about the excitement in the air when a fly ball is hit and baseball fans go crazy. Or maybe there's the crazy breakaway dunk over the NBA's leading scorer. Or there's the last second run back for the game winning touchdown with your favorite football team. The bottom line is there's something in the air that you have to be there to experience and appreciate.

One of my favorite things about going to the ball game is getting dressed to support my team. And one way to get on her good side is to show up in the team paraphernalia, especially if it's supporting her team. For you diehards, would you be selling out? Maybe. But then isn't that what a relationship is all about? Not selling out but compromising, we can't always win or be right.

A side note: one of my closest friends and mentors told me once that if I wanted my relationship with my fiancé to get better I had to realize something; I had a choice of if I wanted to be right or if I wanted to be happy, they don't go hand in hand. And that was good advice. If you don't get it – in arguments no one really wants to be wrong. And so no one wins. To understand her is to understand that you can win by just letting it go. You don't have to be right. You don't want or need to be right…you want to win, correct? If she feels she has made her point and you allow her to feel she is right, even if you feel otherwise, you will find a much happier person in the relationship. Is that cheating? Maybe but it's also a technique for keeping the peace that worked wonders for my marriage.

Back to our regularly scheduled program…going back to our theme, planning. It is a must that you plan accordingly if you want to have a successful outing. Example, you don't want to go to an outdoor park with a forecast for rain and not take an umbrella or jacket. Conversely, you don't want to plan an afternoon game if there isn't going to be a cloud in the sky and the forecast is 110 degrees! You'd look like a complete ignoramus.

Ball games can be pricey, to say the least. I recommend checking on Groupon, or another deal site, for discounted tickets. If you happen to be a procrastinator, sometimes you can get lucky. Some websites offer deeply discounted tickets for same day events. I wouldn't count on that but it may be a viable option if it's a last minute thing. You can also try Craigslist but be very careful because they aren't always authentic. You'd rather pay a little more than get burned.

In going to the ball game, the one sure thing you can count on his horrendous traffic. And maybe there is no way of avoiding it, but then maybe there is. If you plan ahead you can also plan for public or mass transit. For some that may be less than ideal but for others they would have it no other way. Me? I guess I'm indifferent. I prefer to drive but that's only because I know I will want to more in the area and I like the freedom of having my car when and where I want it. But it does come at a fairly steep parking fare. Mass transit can reduce the cost of your outing by at least $20 bucks. And if you've mapped it out, to include the schedule, parking lots, security and stations, you will have less anxiety over it.

In many cases there is a tradition that runs side by side with the game, the tail gate. The tail gate is the party before the game and often times the party after the game. Tail gate parties are a lot of fun! If you've never been to one it's basically just as it sounds. It's an atmosphere of camaraderie and fellowship with a group of people who share the same pride in the institution they have come out to support. To make it plain: there is free food, beer, music and lots of people having a good time, everywhere. If you decide you want to be a part of that, you should plan to arrive at least two hours before game time.

While at the ball game, the most important point to remember is you want to leave an indelible impression on her. Do something to make yourself stand out. What do I recommend? How about a selfie of you and her with a famous statue? Get a picture of the two of you with the team mascot. Make your way to the field after the game. If you must bribe, beg or sneak on the field so you can take a picture there. I guarantee you she has never been on a collegiate or professional field or court.

The ball game date is great for courting single moms too. A lot of times single moms do not have the flexibility in their schedule or budgets to hire babysitters every time they want to go out. But a date like a ball game gives them the option of taking the child along with them. You may have to swallow your pride a bit and share her attention but you come out smelling like roses and looking like a hero as long as you don't make a fuss of it. Be the bigger person.

Chapter Ten

Mix It Up with the Fish

Would you believe up until only a few years ago I had never gone to a zoo? Yes, that means I was forty years old with a 2 year old daughter before I went to the zoo. She and I shared the same look on our faces, both in utter amazement! Too funny. I tell you this because I discovered I wasn't alone, hardly. And while the zoo is indeed fun in its own right, it can be kind of smelly and not necessarily the most pleasant place with hollering and screaming kids running around. You can aim a little higher.

I learned there are many people who have the same story of aquariums, they have never gone to one either. Now aquariums are much more esthetically pleasing. The fish are beautiful and angelic. The enormous tanks are mind boggling and the fish are genuine entertainers. If in your discovery you find she has never been to an aquarium then it will bode well for you, provided she likes fish. Even if she has gone to an aquarium before, or you assume she has, most aquariums have special events, especially during the summer months. They even have discounted tickets.

You can go to eventbite.com to learn more about special events at the aquarium in your area or you can visit the aquarium's website. The special thing about going to the aquarium for an event is it gives you a reason to get dressed up. Do you know how many times I have been told by women that they long for an occasion to get dressed up. Not only them but they want YOU to get dressed up too. They want you to trim your beard, cut your hair, wax your chest or whatever it is you do to look your best.

Now to many this is where we have just come off the rails. I've learned guys today want to be comfortable and there's nothing wrong with that. But, comfort doesn't necessarily buy you any grace with your lady, especially not when you're trying to put your best foot forward. To women, or I should say some women, when you get dressed up it shows them you still care enough to want to get dressed up.

And, you will want to dress nicely if you are going to an event at the aquarium because the crowd tends to be chic and sophisticated. Obviously you aren't going if this doesn't apply to you; but if it applies to her wants then you just may have to bite the bullet. Personally I don't mind an evening of dealing with pretentious posers if it means she had a good time and it advances my agenda of winning her over. Remember, the game is winning...love.

Perhaps what I appreciate most about this date is incredible ambiance the background and setting provides. There is something sensual about dining with fish swimming around you or sharing a cocktail while watching a Beluga whale. The lights are usually dim and there is often entertainment such as a live jazz band or something.

Even if you are not a conversational person, this setting can make it easy and relaxed to just be yourself. The conversation tends to flow freely. And if nothing else you have the fish to talk about as a conversation starter and go to when it becomes slow or uncomfortable. If you go tell Nemo and Dory I said hello!

Chapter Eleven

Touch the Sky with a Balloon Ride

I remember as a young child I always wanted to fly. Of course I had never been in an airplane. Tickets back then were much more expensive than they are today and airplanes were not the preferred vehicle of travel in that time. My only reference to flying was Superman, and my imagination kept me busy. As I grew older and took my first plane ride, it was everything I imagined it would be including the altitude sickness from the first time. But there is little romantic about flying in a plane unless its private jet or you're planning on joining the "mile high club", in which case good luck!

But there are other, sexier ways to fly. Have you ever considered a balloon ride? That's right, a balloon ride. Imagine, what a perfect way to get her alone with you, in a confined space where your breath is sure to be taken away from the fantastic view. It is the thing that separates the men from the boys as a lot of men are fearful of heights – myself included.

The cool thing about a balloon ride is many of them allow you to bring food and small beverages. You can assemble a small picnic (refer to Chapter 1) to enhance the experience. I would not recommend alcohol as the affect would be intensified at the higher altitude but some sparkling grape may work.

What you should expect on the balloon ride is the feeling of weightlessness, a smooth motion as you glide gracefully through the sky. You will get the sense you can reach out and touch the clouds. The view is stunning and the admiration she will have for you allows you an opportunity to pull her in closely. Hold her in your arms reassure her you are her protector.

You see, along with the wonderment of gliding through the air, there is still the cautious awareness of the danger and risk that still looms. It provides for added stimulation and heightening the emotional connection to the moment. By wrapping her in your arms your body language implies you have her back. Sometimes that's all it takes is for a women to feel she isn't in the relationship alone.

When I went on my first balloon ride I wanted to take my own advice. I asked my date to play along with me. We dressed as 1930's bank robbers. I rented an outfit from a local costume rental house. It was a unique experience. The balloon operator got a real kick out of us. He was an older man whose grandfather was a member of a great bank heist in the 50's. Needless to say our outfits prompted a big discussion. He was discrete and only chimed in a few times after we got in the air but our date now had more fuel for the flame, literally.

The day turned to night and the next thing you know as we were coming down the homes with their lights on looked like small tea candles or lightening bugs in the distance. I pulled her in and laid her head against my chest. A tear rolled down her cheek touching my chest. I knew then it was mission accomplished; I had won her heart but she too had won mine.

I encourage you to try any or all of these dating suggestions. Sure, I've offered you more tips and advice than "just" dates but true be told some of us need it; maybe that's you. And while I cannot promise this book will be the remedy for your failing marriage or relationship, I can tell you if there is anything at all left this book can be an effective tool in getting you back on the right track.

I wish you success in your dating efforts. I am hopeful these little tips can help some of you. Please feel free to visit my website for details on more books in the series and feel free to email me details on how I've helped you and your love life.

Also, if you would like to have your ideas considered for future chapters or even potential collaboration please submit them. Send email submissions to deronte.smith@infinity1publishing.com.

Thank you again for your patronage and be well.

www.ingramcontent.com/pod-product-compliance
Lightning Source LLC
Chambersburg PA
CBHW060539030426
42337CB00021B/4351